ENDANGERED AND THREATENED ANIMALS

THE
AMERICAN
ALLIGATOR

A MyReportLinks.com Book

Henry M. Holden

MyReportLinks.com Books

an imprint of

Enslow Publishers, Inc.

Box 398, 40 Industrial Road

Berkeley Heights, NJ 07922

USA

MyReportLinks.com Books, an imprint of Enslow Publishers, Inc. MyReportLinks®
is a registered trademark of Enslow Publishers, Inc.

Copyright © 2003 by Enslow Publishers, Inc.

All rights reserved.

No part of this book may be reproduced by any means
without the written permission of the publisher.

Library of Congress Cataloging-in-Publication Data

Holden, Henry M.
  The American alligator / Henry M. Holden.
     p. cm. — (Endangered and threatened animals)
Summary: Discusses what American alligators are, why they are
endangered, what their current status is, and what is being done to help
them. Includes Internet links to Web sites related to American
alligators.
Includes bibliographical references (p.   ).
  ISBN 0-7660-5117-X
 1. American alligator—Juvenile literature. 2. Endangered
species—Juvenile literature. [1. Alligators. 2. Endangered species.]
I. Title. II. Series.
QL666.C925 H638 2003
597.98'4—dc21

                                   2002014861

Printed in the United States of America

10 9 8 7 6 5 4 3 2

To Our Readers:
Through the purchase of this book, you and your library gain access to the Report Links that specifically back
up this book.
The Publisher will provide access to the Report Links that back up this book and will keep these Report Links
up to date on **www.myreportlinks.com** for five years from the book's first publication date.
We have done our best to make sure all Internet addresses in this book were active and appropriate when we
went to press. However, the author and the Publisher have no control over, and assume no liability for, the
material available on those Internet sites or on other Web sites they may link to.
The usage of the MyReportLinks.com Books Web site is subject to the terms and conditions stated on the
Usage Policy Statement on **www.myreportlinks.com.**
A password may be required to access the Report Links that back up this book. The password is found on the
bottom of page 4 of this book.
Any comments or suggestions can be sent by e-mail to comments@myreportlinks.com or to the address on
the back cover.

Photo Credits: © Corel Corporation, pp. 1, 3, 11, 25, 28, 38; Henry M. Holden, pp. 22, 26, 32, 37;
John Bavaro, p. 18; Louisiana State University, p. 16; LSU AgCenter, p. 31; MyReportLinks.com
Books, p. 4; *National Geographic*, p. 23; NatureWorks, p. 19; Pictor International, p. 34, PictureQuest,
p. 41; University of Florida, pp. 12, 14, 20, 21; Timothy O'Keefe/PictureQuest, p. 10; U. S. Fish &
Wildlife Service, p. 43; William Folsom/National Oceanic & Atmospheric Administration, p. 34.

Cover Photo: Jan Tove Johansson/PictureQuest

Contents

MyReportLinks.com Books
Great Books, Great Links, Great for Research!

MyReportLinks.com Books present the information you need to learn about your report subject. In addition, they show you where to go on the Internet for more information. The pre-evaluated Report Links that back up this book are kept up to date on **www.myreportlinks.com**. With the purchase of a MyReportLinks.com Books title, you and your library gain access to the Report Links that specifically back up that book. The Report Links save hours of research time and link to dozens—even hundreds—of Web sites, source documents, and photos related to your report topic.

Please see "To Our Readers" on the Copyright page for important information about this book, the MyReportLinks.com Books Web site, and the Report Links that back up this book.

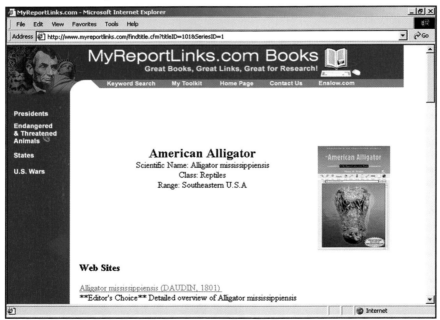

Access:

The Publisher will provide access to the Report Links that back up this book and will try to keep these Report Links up to date on our Web site for five years from the book's first publication date. Please enter **EAA1474** if asked for a password.

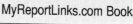 MyReportLinks.com Books

Go!

Report Links

The Internet sites described below can be accessed at
http://www.myreportlinks.com

▶ *Alligator mississippiensis* (DAUDIN, 1801)   *EDITOR'S CHOICE
This Web site provides a detailed overview of *Alligator mississippiensis*, along with distribution maps and a number of images. You will also learn about conservation efforts and miscellaneous facts.

Link to this Internet site from http://www.myreportlinks.com

▶ U.S. Fish and Wildlife Service: Species Information   *EDITOR'S CHOICE
At the U.S. Fish and Wildlife Service Web site you will find links to the Endangered Species Act, the federal list of endangered and threatened wildlife and plants, and other resources on endangered species.

Link to this Internet site from http://www.myreportlinks.com

▶ NatureWorks: American Alligator   *EDITOR'S CHOICE
NatureWorks provides a profile of the American alligator, where you can learn about its physical characteristics, habitat, diet, and behavior.

Link to this Internet site from http://www.myreportlinks.com

▶ American Museum of Natural History   *EDITOR'S CHOICE
The American Museum of Natural History explores many endangered species, including the American crocodile. Here you will find basic facts and links to definitions of terminology.

Link to this Internet site from http://www.myreportlinks.com

▶ Everglades National Park   *EDITOR'S CHOICE
This site has a lot of information about the American alligator, including what to do if you encounter one in the wild! There are links to pictures of 'gator holes' and a page on how to tell alligators and crocodiles apart.

Link to this Internet site from http://www.myreportlinks.com

▶ Creature World: American Alligator   *EDITOR'S CHOICE
PBS's Creature World presents interesting facts about the American alligator. Here you will learn what you would be able to do if you were an alligator.

Link to this Internet site from http://www.myreportlinks.com

The Internet sites described below can be accessed at
http://www.myreportlinks.com

▶ *Alligator mississippiensis*
At this Web site you will learn about the American alligator. Learn about its classification, physical characteristics, habitat, and behavior.

Link to this Internet site from http://www.myreportlinks.com

▶ **Amazing Animals: American Alligator**
The American alligator can be found in many southern states between Texas and Florida. This Web site provides a brief description of the American alligator's physical characteristics and habitat.

Link to this Internet site from http://www.myreportlinks.com

▶ **American Alligator**
This overview of the American alligator discusses its physical characteristics, vocalizations during breeding season, habitat, and range.

Link to this Internet site from http://www.myreportlinks.com

▶ **The American Alligator**
The American Alligator Web site contains information about American alligator populations of the past and present, their feeding habits, and safety tips.

Link to this Internet site from http://www.myreportlinks.com

▶ **America Zoo: American Alligator**
The America Zoo Web site describes the origin of the alligator's name, where it lives, its habitat, physical description, behavior, and reproductive cycle.

Link to this Internet site from http://www.myreportlinks.com

▶ **Animal Bytes**
Animal Bytes, part of the Seaworld Web site, provides basic facts about the American alligator.

Link to this Internet site from http://www.myreportlinks.com

The Internet sites described below can be accessed at
http://www.myreportlinks.com

▶ Bagheera

The Bagheera Web site is dedicated to educating individuals about endangered species, the extinction crisis, pollution, habitat loss, over exploitation, and other issues.

Link to this Internet site from http://www.myreportlinks.com

▶ BBC News

This interesting site describes how alligators are a close, living relative of dinosaurs, and how scientists have been studying their breathing methods to learn about how dinosaurs may have breathed.

Link to this Internet site from http://www.myreportlinks.com

▶ Crocodile Specialist Group

Learn about how conservation efforts have helped to save all of the crocodilian species. There are also links to their newsletter publications, which have current information.

Link to this Internet site from http://www.myreportlinks.com

▶ Crocodilians: Natural History and Conservation

Learn about the twenty-three species of living crocodilians, including the American alligator. This site is full of information, such as how alligators and crocodiles communicate with each other, as well as downloadable files of the sounds they make.

Link to this Internet site from http://www.myreportlinks.com

▶ Endangered Species

At this site you will find links to the endangered species list, laws and policies, and species recovery programs. There are also links to international organizations dedicated to endangered animals.

Link to this Internet site from http://www.myreportlinks.com

▶ Gatorland

This theme park's Web site is a fun site for photos of baby crocodiles and alligators.

Link to this Internet site from http://www.myreportlinks.com

Report Links

 The Internet sites described below can be accessed at
http://www.myreportlinks.com

▶ Louisiana Agriculture

At the Louisiana Agriculture Web site you can read about what happens to alligators before and after they hatch, and how the alligator population in the wild has increased.

Link to this Internet site from http://www.myreportlinks.com

▶ Louisiana's Amazing White Alligators

White alligators are a rare occurrence in nature. This Web site describes their physical characteristics, why they are threatened, and the conservation efforts to save them.

Link to this Internet site from http://www.myreportlinks.com

▶ *National Geographic*

This fascinating *National Geographic* Web site examines the history of a super crocodile that lived 110 million years ago. There are links to maps, an interactive game, and biographies of the scientific explorers.

Link to this Internet site from http://www.myreportlinks.com

▶ National Parks Conservation Association

At the National Parks Conservation Association Web site you can read about the conservation effort to help protect the American crocodile, which is endangered. Click on the "read more" link at the bottom of the page to access more information.

Link to this Internet site from http://www.myreportlinks.com

▶ Nile Crocodile

Nile crocodiles live in groups of up to one hundred and work in groups to catch food. Learn more about this reptile on this site.

Link to this Internet site from http://www.myreportlinks.com

▶ *NOVA* Online

From PBS's *NOVA* Online, this Web site has an interview with a crocodile specialist, a 'clickable croc' map, and a list of the twenty-three different types of crocodilians.

Link to this Internet site from http://www.myreportlinks.com

Any comments? Contact us: **comments@myreportlinks.com**

Report Links

▶ *OneWorld Magazine*

The Crocodile Files Web site allows you to hear crocodile sounds. Click on "smart reptiles" to read about how they are the most intelligent reptiles.

Link to this Internet site from http://www.myreportlinks.com

▶ Vancouver Aquarium

The Vancouver Aquarium Web site contains interesting information about crocodilians, such as the fact that they can go for one month without eating.

Link to this Internet site from http://www.myreportlinks.com

▶ The Virtual Zoo

ThinkQuest provides a brief overview of the differences between the American and Chinese alligator. You will also learn how crocodiles differ from alligators.

Link to this Internet site from http://www.myreportlinks.com

▶ The Visible Alligator Skull

This site explains the alligator skull project. It also contains information about the evolutionary history of alligators and the differences between alligators and crocodiles.

Link to this Internet site from http://www.myreportlinks.com

▶ *World Almanac for Kids Online* Alligator

The *World Almanac for Kids Online* provides a quick overview of the American alligator.

Link to this Internet site from http://www.myreportlinks.com

▶ Yak's Corner

At the Yak's Corner Web site you can explore the characteristics of the Chinese alligator. These smaller cousins of the American alligator are endangered, with less than one thousand of them left in China.

Link to this Internet site from http://www.myreportlinks.com

American Alligator Facts

▶ **Reptilia Family**
Alligatoridae

▶ **Genus**
Alligator

▶ **Species**
Alligator mississippiensis
(mississippiensis means
"of the Mississippi River")

▶ **Federal Status**
No longer endangered or
threatened, but still being
monitored.

▶ **Range**
Southeastern
United States
AL, AR, FL, GA, LA,
MS, NC, OK, SC, TX

▶ **Habitat**
Freshwater lakes,
marshlands

▶ **Average Length**
Up to 19 feet
(5.79 meters)

▶ **Average Weight**
Up to 500 pounds
(226.8 kilograms)

▶ **Life Span**
40 to 70 years

▶ **Threats to Survival**
Habitat destruction,
waterborne toxic
chemicals

▶ **Closely-Related Species**
American crocodile,
Chinese alligator

▶ **Teeth**
Varies from 74 to 80

▶ **Incubation Period**
An average of 65 days.

Prehistoric Monsters

Alligators look like prehistoric monsters. They are the closest, living creatures we have to dinosaurs.[1] The alligator and crocodile belong to a large family of reptiles called crocodilians. Crocodilians and dinosaurs belong to a group called archosaurs. This means "ruling reptiles."

Alligators lived with dinosaurs for about 230 million years. About 65 million years ago, the dinosaurs vanished from the earth. Some scientists believe that the earth's temperature became too cold for them. Most dinosaurs lived only on land. They were too big to hibernate in dens or caves. The dinosaurs could not adapt to the change and died. The alligators, however, adapted to the changing climate. They survived floods, droughts, and other changes in the weather.

▼ The American alligator's ability to adapt to the changing climate has kept it alive for millions of years.

Alligators are cold-blooded animals. They control their body temperature through outside sources. That is why they are often seen sunning themselves on logs or on banks near water. Alligators lie in the sun to raise their body temperature. They may open their mouths to cool off. The large, exposed, wet surface lets body heat escape.

When it gets too hot, alligators may cool off in the water. They may stay almost completely underwater when the air is cold. They will only expose their eyes and nose.

Alligators have no natural enemies after they grow to about four feet (1.22 m) long. Only people and larger alligators are their enemies. Heavy hunting for their hides

Crocodile Action Plan 29 - Microsoft Internet Explorer

File   Edit   View   Favorites   Tools   Help

Address http://www.flmnh.ufl.edu/natsci/herpetology/act-plan/a-plan29.htm

Chinese alligator, *Alligator sinensis*.
Myrna Watanabe photo. Copyright © 1996 M. Watanabe.

[Crocodile Action Plan Chinese Alligator Page]---- [Crocodile Photo Gallery]---- [Crocodile Specialist Group]

Internet

▲ *The Chinese alligator is virtually extinct in the wilds of its native China, however different programs have allowed for a healthy captive population to exist.*

drove the alligators to the edge of extinction. Extinction means there are no more of the species living. Today only two species of alligator remain: the American alligator and the Chinese alligator, which lives in eastern China.

In 1973, the U.S. Congress put the alligator on the endangered species list. An endangered species is one that is dying out. Conservation efforts saved the alligator, and today it is no longer endangered. Since the alligator looks like the crocodile, the alligator is still listed as threatened to help protect the crocodile. The crocodile is in danger of extinction. Only about five hundred are left.[2]

However, the alligator now faces new threats. People are building houses and malls on their habitat. An animal's *habitat* is where it lives. As people continue to push the alligator out of its home, it becomes a danger to them. Alligators are forced to seek water in swimming pools and lakes where people swim.

Other animals native to the region are also in trouble, because their homes are disappearing. In Florida, the crocodile is losing its habitat to people. Only one small piece of its habitat is left in South Florida.

Scientists agree that water pollution is harming the alligator's eggs, as well. If people understand that pesticides can kill baby alligators, and if people work to reduce use of pesticides, then alligators can be saved. People must find a way to coexist with alligators, so they do not harm one another.

Profile of the Alligator

Alligators are North America's largest reptiles. They look like large lizards, with short legs and long tails. When Spanish explorers first saw alligators, they called them "el lagarto," which means "the lizard." The English word became "aligarto," and then "alligator."

Crocodile Specialist Group Q - Microsoft Internet Explorer

File Edit View Favorites Tools Help

Address http://www.flmnh.ufl.edu/natsci/herpetology/crocs/crocsq.htm

The Nile crocodile, _Crocodylus niloticus_.
F. Wayne King photo. Copyright © 1996

[Return to CSG Meetings]---- [Crocodile Photo Gallery]---- [Crocodile Specialist Group]

Internet

▲ Although crocodiles look very similar to alligators, there are some physical differences. For instance, you can see one tooth of the crocodile's lower jaw when the animal's mouth is closed. This is not so with the alligator.

People often mistake the alligator for its close relative—the crocodile. Alligators look like crocodiles, but there are differences. On the lower jaw of crocodiles, one tooth on each side is visible when the animal's mouth is closed. When an alligator's mouth is closed, its lower teeth are not visible.

Alligators have a broad snout. Crocodiles have a narrow snout. Alligators have darker hides than crocodiles. If you hear one of these big reptiles bellowing, it is an alligator. Crocodiles do not bellow.

▶ Physical Characteristics

Prehistoric alligators were up to thirty-six feet (10.97 m) long.[1] On average, modern alligators grow 6 to 13 feet (1.8 to 3.96 m) long. One captured in Lake Apopka, Florida, was 17 feet, 5 inches (5 m).[2] The largest alligator ever captured was 19 feet, 2 inches (5.8 m).[3] About half of the length of an alligator is its huge tail.

Male alligators grow faster, and are larger, than females. Females will grow to about nine feet (2.7 m) and two hundred pounds (90.7 kg). Males will grow to about thirteen feet (3.96 m) and weigh over five hundred pounds (226.8 kg). Some can live almost as long as people, over seventy years.

As big and as strong as they are, alligators have a brain the size of a lima bean.[4] This limits their thinking to biting, eating, and mating.

Alligators have tough, black, scaly hides. They have many small peaks or spines across their back and tail. The scales on their bellies are an ivory color.

There are white, or albino, alligators, but they are rare. Fewer than fifty white alligators are in captivity. An adult has never been seen in the wild, and they have only been

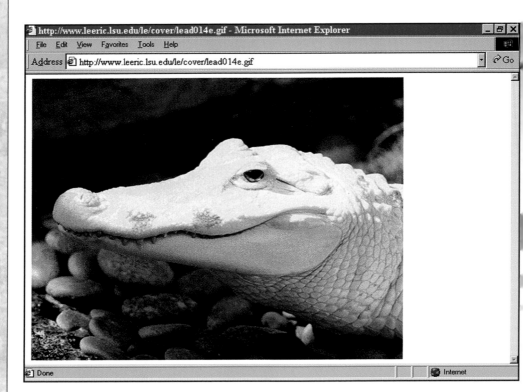

▲ *In 1987, a nest containing eighteen white alligators was found in Louisiana. This was the first discovery of such animals in recorded history, although Eastern mythology mentions white alligators as symbols of good luck.*

found in Louisiana. The easily-seen, white hatchlings must beware of predators and the sun. If its skin is burnt, it will likely die.[5]

Alligators are comfortable on land and in the water. In the water, they use their powerful tail to help them swim. They swish their tail with back-and-forth movements. Most of the time they glide slowly through the water, holding their legs against their body. They can "tail walk" like dolphins do. This means they can hold their head and body vertically out of the water to look around and breathe.

Alligators have four legs that extend from their sides. On land, they walk along the ground with their huge front and hind limbs. They have huge, clawed feet. Their front feet have five separate toes, and their back feet have four partially-webbed toes. Alligators normally walk with their bodies off the ground; their ankles twist to allow their legs to be almost underneath their body. No other reptiles move in this way. They are capable of short bursts of speed. This allows them to catch prey. Some small alligators can run at speeds of ten miles per hour (16.1 km/h).[6] They are too big to give chase if they miss the prey.

Alligators can open their big mouths and grab prey underwater. They do not have lips, so even when their mouths are closed, water leaks in. Alligators do this without getting water in their lungs or stomach.

When an alligator dives underwater, a flap of skin closes over its throat. It can open its mouth to capture food but not swallow water. Another flap of skin covers its ears, and special muscles, like valves, close its nostrils. A membrane, called a third eyelid, covers its eyes but still allows it to see.

The jaws of an alligator are very powerful. They can snap shut with three thousand pounds of pressure per square inch. Alligators have large, spike-like teeth. These can smash hard-shelled turtles or crush bones in larger prey. They use their jaws and teeth to crush and tear apart their prey. Alligators cannot chew their food so they swallow food completely or in chunks.

Alligator's teeth are thick-walled cones on the outside of their jaws. The teeth are not embedded in the jawbone. This means they can break off. Alligators will lose their

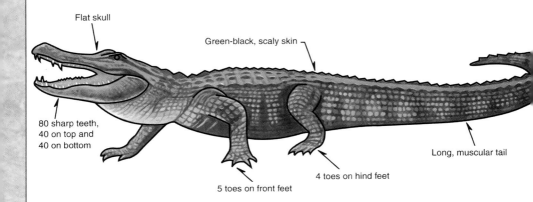

Flat skull

Green-black, scaly skin

80 sharp teeth,
40 on top and
40 on bottom

Long, muscular tail

4 toes on hind feet

5 toes on front feet

teeth many times, and always regrow new ones. They have about seventy-four to eighty teeth at one time.

▶ Eye Shine

Alligators have eyes similar to those of cats. On the backs of their eyes are layers of cells that gather and reflect any light. This helps them see at night. Their vertical pupils are only slits in the daytime. At night, these widen to allow them to see well in the dark.

An alligator's olive-green eyes will glow in the dark when light strikes them. Their eyes reflect blazing red, and they do not blink. With powerful searchlights, the eye shine can be seen for 200 to 300 yards (182.9 to 274.3 m). Scientists count alligators at night by counting the glowing eyes. The eyes of the adult male shine red. The eyes of the females and young shine greenish or bluish yellow.[7]

Alligators' eyes are on the tops of their heads and close together. This allows them to have excellent depth perception. Their nose and ears are also on the top of their head. This way they can see, hear, and smell as they float almost unseen on the water.

Communications

The alligators "talk" with sounds, motions, odors, and by touch. The babies "talk" with each other while still in their shells.[8] Alligators use their deep, roaring voices to call a mate, to scare off another alligator, and to find each other at night.

Habitat

Alligators' habitat is the freshwater swamps, lakes, marshlands, and rivers. They live in the Southeast, where the winters are mild. They range from central Texas and Florida to North Carolina.

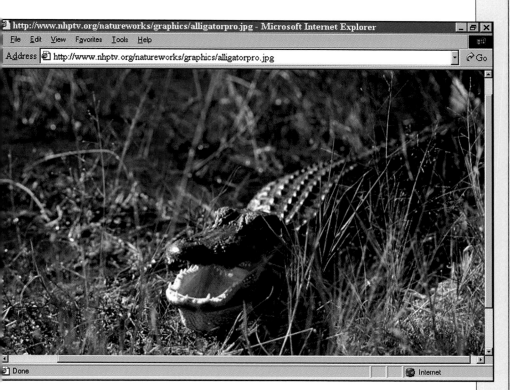

http://www.nhptv.org/natureworks/graphics/alligatorpro.jpg - Microsoft Internet Explorer

File   Edit   View   Favorites   Tools   Help

Address http://www.nhptv.org/natureworks/graphics/alligatorpro.jpg   Go

Done   Internet

The powerful jaws of an American alligator can bite down with three thousand pounds of pressure per square inch.

When the weather turns cold, alligators dig dens at the water's edge. This gives them warmth, shelter, and protection. These dens also give refuge for other animals, such as fish, frogs, and turtles. During dry periods, the den may be the only source of water. Alligators dig these holes using both their snout and tail. Once these holes dry out, however, alligators cross land to find another body of water.

▷ Diet

Alligators are carnivores. They will eat whatever they can catch if they are hungry. This includes slow-moving fish, birds, mammals, frogs, and snakes. Alligators will also eat

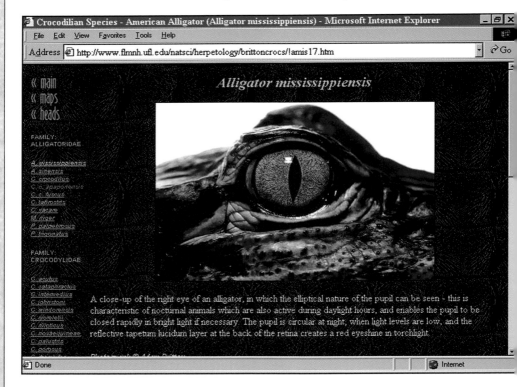

The alligator's shiny eyes are located on the top of its head. This allows the animal to have excellent depth perception as well as see while mostly emerged in water.

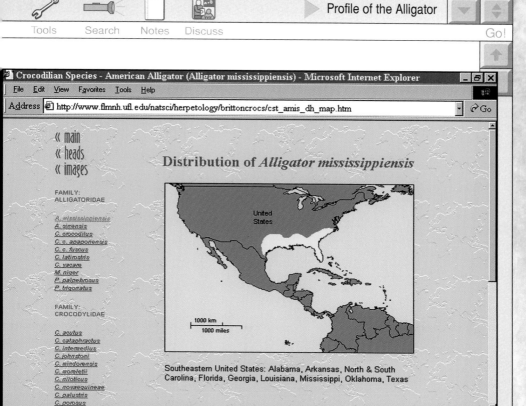

Crocodilian Species - American Alligator (Alligator mississippiensis) - Microsoft Internet Explorer

File   Edit   View   Favorites   Tools   Help

Address http://www.flmnh.ufl.edu/natsci/herpetology/brittoncrocs/cst_amis_dh_map.htm

« main
« heads
« images

FAMILY:
ALLIGATORIDAE

A. mississippiensis
A. sinensis
C. crocodilus
C. c. apaporiensis
C. c. fuscus
C. latirostris
C. yacare
M. niger
P. palpebrosus
P. trigonatus

FAMILY:
CROCODYLIDAE

C. acutus
C. cataphractus
C. intermedius
C. johnstoni
C. mindorensis
C. moreletii
C. niloticus
C. novaeguineae
C. palustris
C. porosus

Distribution of *Alligator mississippiensis*

United States

1000 km
1000 miles

Southeastern United States: Alabama, Arkansas, North & South
Carolina, Florida, Georgia, Louisiana, Mississippi, Oklahoma, Texas

Internet

American alligators live in the freshwater lakes, marshlands, swamps, and rivers of the southeastern United States. These states include Alabama, Arkansas, the Carolinas, Florida, Georgia, Louisiana, Mississippi, Oklahoma, and Texas.

carrion (dead animals) if they are hungry.[9] Alligators may eat small dogs and other pets. They sometimes spring out of water to catch birds.[10] Up to 60 percent of their food intake may be converted to fat.[11] Food is stored as fat in the animal's tail, back, and elsewhere in the body.

Alligators hunt by hiding until the prey comes close to them. One method they use is to imitate a log. The alligator will lie very still up close to the bank of the water. A rabbit or other small animal will step out on the "log" to drink. The instant the animal steps off its back, the

By using their strong tails, alligators are able to catch prey, such as a bird, in midair.

alligator explodes into action. It will catch the animal faster than the eye can follow. "I have never seen one miss," said LeRoy Overstreet, an alligator hunter. "I have seen rabbits walk from one end of the log to the other and drink and wash several times. The gator always lies perfectly still until the instant the animal leaves its back."[12]

In the wild, alligators do not eat when it gets cold. They begin to lose their appetite when it gets below 80°F (26.7°C). They stop feeding altogether below 73°F (22.8°C).[13] The alligator's cold-blooded system is very efficient. The animal can survive the winter on its fat reserves.

▶ Mating

Females are about ten years old before they mate. The mating season for alligators takes place during April and May. By ten years old they are about six feet (1.8 m) long. A male, or "bull" alligator, begins bellowing in the spring to attract females. This bellow also warns others to stay away. This roar is heard over great distances. The deep, throaty sound is similar to the roar of a lion. The message is the same. "I am here . . . I am big . . . I am the boss . . . I am the lion of the marsh."[14]

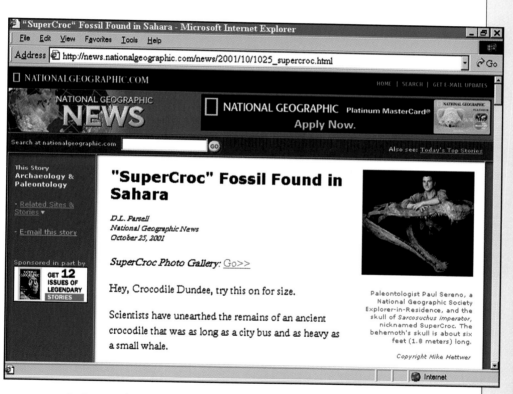

Sarcosuchus imperator, *otherwise known as Super Croc, shares common ancestry with today's alligators. This animal lived along the rivers of Africa 110 million years ago, although there is record of even older crocodilian species dating from 230 million years ago.*

Bull alligators will fight to see who are the biggest and the toughest in the swamp. The winners get to court the females or "sow" alligators.

Alligators are vicious fighters. They tear and bite at their opponents. They will fight until one dies or one retreats, badly injured.

Alligators mate underwater. After mating, the female will carry the eggs for about two months. The female will build a nest of marsh plants in June or July. She will pile the plants in a mound up to three feet (.91 m) high and ten feet (3.05 m) across. She scrapes the nest together with her feet. Then she lays her eggs at night. She will deposit between thirty and sixty eggs.

The decaying plants create heat to incubate the eggs. The eggs have a tough, leathery shell and take about two to three months to hatch. Females lay eggs only once a year, but they will lay eggs for twenty to thirty years.[15]

Often, predators will destroy the nest. About 70 percent of the eggs are lost to predators during incubation.[16] Usually, the alligator will build the nest above the water. Sometimes floods or heavy rains will destroy the nest and kill the eggs. Only 10 percent of the hatchlings survive to measure four feet long.[17]

Adults, especially females, often guard the nests. The female will attack anything she thinks is a threat to her eggs. Scientists think this is one reason alligators have survived since the age of the dinosaurs.[18]

The temperature of the nest will decide the sex of the hatchlings. Temperatures above 86°F (30°C) will create all males. Below this temperature, all females will hatch. No one knows how or why this way of determining male and female evolved.[19]

Tools Search Notes Discuss Go!

▶ Hatchlings

All eggs in a nest will hatch at the same time. The hatchling has an "egg tooth" on top of its snout to help open the egg. When its head pops out, it immediately starts chirping. Soon all the hatchlings are chirping. This is a signal to the mother that it is time to leave the nest. The entire brood leaves the nest at the same time.

If the hatchlings cannot get out on their own, the female digs open the nest and sets them free. If an egg does not hatch properly, she may gently break the egg in her massive jaws to help the hatchling get out. She may even carry some hatchlings to the water in her mouth.

▲ It is advised that anyone stay away from a pod. Mother alligators are extremely protective of their young. They will attack anything that may threaten the safety of the pod, including humans, herons, and male alligators.

▲ *The bright-yellow bands lining the backs of baby alligators help them hide from predators. This coloring acts as camouflage, allowing them to blend into their surroundings.*

She pulls her tongue down to form a pouch for them. Once in the water, she opens her jaws, and shakes her head gently side to side. This encourages her babies to start swimming.[20]

Hatchlings instinctively begin to feed on crayfish, snails, and water bugs.[21] Young alligators will eat insects, tadpoles, and frogs. As they grow larger and stronger, they will eat larger fish and small mammals.

Once hatched, the babies form pods. A pod may include babies from others nests. This provides protection in numbers when they are most helpless. The nearest female will respond quickly if they begin calling because of danger. A female alligator may care for her young until they are two years old.

New hatchlings are miniature versions of their parents. They are about eight inches long and weigh about two ounces. They have tiny, needle-like teeth. Large fish, turtles, birds, and raccoons prey on the hatchlings.[22] To help them survive, they have bright-yellow cross bands on a black background. This is their camouflage. These colors blend with the sunlit grasses. As the baby gets older, these markings will fade. The yellow banding turns olive-brown and black.

Hatchlings do not grow quickly in the wild. They do not eat when it gets cold, so, the hatchlings are not very big by the following spring.[23] Young wild alligators may grow up to one foot (.3 m) every year until they are fully-grown.[24]

Alligator Hunting

Alligators are an important part of the culture in the southeastern United States. American Indians were the first people to hunt alligators for their hide and meat. They believed the teeth of an alligator were magical and could prevent snakebite. They thought alligators were immune to the bite of poisonous snakes. The native people made leather clothing and musical instruments, such as drums, from the hide. They valued the alligator, and took only what they needed to live.

The alligator was an important resource for people in the eighteenth century. Hunters used its hide to make boots, shoes, and saddles. Its oil was used to grease machinery. The hunters also ate the meat. There were

▼ *Throughout history, people have hunted the alligator to make products such as shoes and purses.*

millions of alligators then, and few hunters. There was no danger of the alligator dying out.

▷ Alligator Products

The only part of the alligator that has market value is the hide on the belly, legs, and underside of the tail. The hides of these parts were used to make shoes and saddles for the Confederate troops during the Civil War. After the war, demand dropped off, because there was no way to preserve the leather for long periods.

In the late 1800s, a tanning process came along that made the hide soft and long lasting. Alligator leather became popular. Stores in large cities began selling these goods. The demand for alligator boots, handbags, and shoes spread to Europe. This began the mass hunting of alligators for their hides. In just ten years, people killed over 2.5 million alligators in Florida, alone.[1] This slaughter would go on for almost one hundred years.

As the demand for these hides grew, the killing got worse. In one year, twelve men terminated four thousand alligators.[2] Between 1880 and 1894, 2.5 million alligators died mainly for profit.[3]

In the first decade of the twentieth century, Louisiana and Florida supplied almost half the hides to the market.[4] The slaughter continued. Each year, the South was producing 126 tons (128.02 metric tons) of hides.[5] Most of these hides came from Florida. In 1943, the alligators' declining numbers led to a new law. Hunters could only kill alligators over four feet (1.22 m) long. This did not help stop the slaughter. In 1954, the law was changed. Hunters could now only kill alligators over six feet (1.83 m) long. This still did not stop the killing. The alligators were losing ground.

After the hunters killed all the large alligators, they came after the smaller ones. The smaller ones did not have a chance to lay their eggs. This meant there were no alligators to replace the ones killed. Even baby alligators were not safe. Hunters captured the babies and sold them to pet stores in the North. As the babies grew, they became too big for a home. People would flush them down the toilet. These alligators never had a chance to grow up and lay eggs. The alligator was on the road to extinction.

By the 1940s, alligator leather was a big business. In Louisiana, one company was tanning almost 1,500 hides a month.[6] Stores around the world were selling these leather goods. The hunters went too far. If all the alligators killed in Louisiana were placed head to tail, they would cover a distance of over forty miles (64.37 km). At one time there were millions of alligators in the area. By the 1960s, Louisiana had less than one hundred thousand left.[7]

▶ Conservation

The first serious efforts to save the American alligator began in 1961. First, Florida, then Louisiana banned hunting. This created an illegal market for hides. Poachers, the people who catch and kill animals protected by law, were hunting more alligators. The price for hides continued to go up. This caused more poaching. The alligator was near extinction.

Because of a mistake in state laws, the police were not able to stop the trade of illegal hides. In 1967, the American alligator was placed on the first state endangered species list. However, this still did not stop the killing right away.

In 1973, Congress stepped in to save the alligator. The Endangered Species Act gave federal protection to all

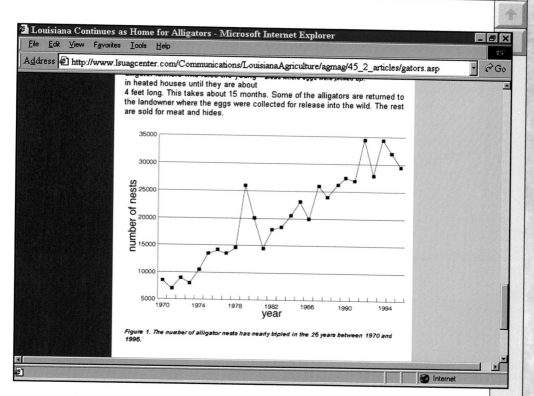

in heated houses until they are about
4 feet long. This takes about 15 months. Some of the alligators are returned to
the landowner where the eggs were collected for release into the wild. The rest
are sold for meat and hides.

Figure 1. The number of alligator nests has nearly tripled in the 25 years between 1970 and 1995.

▲ Between 1970 and 1995, the number of alligator nests occurring in the wild nearly tripled.

alligators. People caught killing them would go to jail or get heavy fines. This soon stopped almost all the poaching.

With alligator hunting illegal, poachers began killing crocodiles. They hunted them almost to extinction. Crocodiles became an endangered species in 1979.

Today, alligators are back in large numbers. There are more than one million wild alligators in Florida. There are another two million in Louisiana.[8] They are no longer listed as endangered or threatened. However, they are still protected where they live. The U.S. Fish and Wildlife Service regulates the legal trade in alligator hides. This is to protect the crocodile and other threatened species in the area.

▶ Legal Hunting

Alligator hunting is now legal in some states. This is because there are too many in some areas. States have different rules for hunting. It depends on the number of alligators in the state. For some hunters, this means extra money for their daily expenses. Each state controls the methods of hunting.

There are several legal methods of hunting alligators. Some states allow live traps, hooks, or the use of harpoons. Other states allow the use of firearms or "bang sticks."

A bang stick is like a gun with a blank bullet inside. When the alligator is pulled to the edge of the boat on a harpoon cable, the hunter knocks the end of the bang stick into its head. This kills the animal instantly.[9]

Since 1988, Florida has allowed some sport hunting on public lakes. The state holds a lottery for the 1,500 permits. Each permit allows the hunter to take two

▲ Alligator hunting has become legal in Florida, Louisiana, and Texas. This is because alligator populations have become overcrowded in some areas.

alligators. Almost eight thousand people apply for these permits each year.

In Florida, alligators may be hunted at night. The only legal way is with a harpoon, bow, bang stick, or crossbow. Baited hooks and firearms are illegal.[10]

Hunting alligators in Louisiana is a business and a sport. The state is the leading producer of hides. It sells about 75 percent of all wild alligator hides in the world.

There are about 4.5 million acres of alligator habitat in Louisiana. About 3.5 million acres are wetlands. This is where most of the alligators live. Most of this is privately owned.[11] Almost all of the land is part of the alligator-hunting program.[12]

In order to hunt, a person must own the property or show written permission to hunt on the property. The hunter also needs a permit from the state. Alligators are dangerous, so the hunter must also have a guide along. Night hunting is not allowed. Most alligators are taken by hanging a baited hook over the water's surface. The alligator is killed by shotgun while it is hanging on the hook. Shotguns and bow hunting are legal ways of killing alligators in Louisiana.[13]

Texas allows hunting in four state parks. About one thousand people apply for permits. Most hunters use baited hooks to catch the alligators. Harpoons and bows may also be used. They kill the alligator afterward with a shotgun. Killing alligators with rifles and handguns is illegal in Texas.

Some states allow hunting, because alligator farms have increased the number of wild alligators. The farms raise alligators for their hides and meat. They also return some to the wild.

Chapter 4

Alligator Farming

The first alligator farm opened in Florida in 1893. Until the 1960s, these farms were like zoos. People just came to see the animals.

In the 1960s, scientists saw alligator farms as an answer to poaching. If farms could grow enough hides, there would be no need to kill wild alligators illegally. Several states created alligator management programs. These programs have increased the number of wild alligators. The programs allow the collection of wild alligator eggs.

▶ Egg Collecting

Only Louisiana, Florida, and Texas allow egg collecting. In all other states, it is illegal to take eggs from the wild.[1]

Each July, egg collectors bravely head out to the marshes and swamps to collect alligator eggs. They often use helicopters to spot the nests. They use

◀ Egg collectors must enter swamps, such as the one pictured here, where alligators are most likely to build their nests, in order to gather eggs.

Tools   Search   Notes   Discuss   Go!

airboats to go deep into the swamps, sometimes at night. When they find a nest, they have the dangerous job of collecting the eggs. One person will remove the eggs, while another person uses a big pole to keep the alligator away from its nest.

Alligators produce more eggs in the wild than they do on farms. However, predators, like raccoons, eat many of the eggs. Eggs are also lost in floods, and if it gets too hot, they dry out. Collecting the eggs and hatching them on farms insures that most will live.

Alligator Farms

On the farm, the eggs incubate in warm tanks inside buildings. They hatch in September. The young alligators live in buildings that feel like their natural habitat. They have a controlled climate and water temperature. They float in their stalls and eat pellets of specially-prepared food.

Instead of mud, the alligators live in plastic-lined pools. This prevents damage to their hides. Any damage or bruises would decrease the value of the hides when they go to market.

When the alligators are three (.91 m) to five feet (1.52 m) in length, some are returned to the swamps. This will ensure that there are enough wild alligators for the ecosystem. Some are harvested when they reach three feet (.91 m). This is the ideal size for making hides into watchbands. The larger alligators usually make bigger items, such as handbags and boots.

The buildings are warm all-year long, and the alligators grow very quickly in that controlled environment. The farms can double the alligator's normal growth rate. They are sometimes nearly four feet (1.22 m) long by the

following spring.[2] It takes about four to five years to reach that length in the wild.

Alligators born on farms continue to grow during the winter. Wild alligators do not grow during the winter. They lie resting in cold weather. Farms produce market-sized alligators about five to six feet (1.52 to 1.83 m) in less than three years.

The farm is a better place for alligators to grow. In the wild, only 17 percent of the alligators reach the length of four feet (1.22 m). This is due to cannibalism and predators.[3] Farm-raised alligators reach mating size at about six to seven years old. In the wild, it is about ten years old.

▶ **Farming Programs**

Today, six states allow alligator farms: Alabama, Georgia, Louisiana, Florida, Mississippi, and Texas.[4] Louisiana began alligator farming in 1986. Louisiana leads the alligator farm market. They have about sixty-four alligator farms. They raise about half a million alligators.[5]

Louisiana supplies about 70 percent of the world's hide supply. In 1998, it shipped 142,000 hides. Most go to Italy or France. About fifty thousand hides were sold in the United States.[6]

One firm in Louisiana tans about twelve thousand hides a year. About half the hides come from farms.[7] The rest come from legal hunting. The farm alligators allowed the market to grow. With enough farm hides available, there is no need to poach wild alligators. Careful tagging, tracking, and policing of the hides also keep poaching down. Now it is very hard to buy or sell illegal hides.[8]

Florida began alligator farming in 1985. It has about thirty alligator farms. They grow about three hundred thousand pounds (1,361 kg) of meat a year. They also sell

Alligator farms located in Alabama, Georgia, Louisiana, Florida, Mississippi, and Texas, have helped to eliminate illegal hunting of the American alligator and return the crocodilian's population to healthy numbers.

over fifteen thousand hides a year. Hide prices vary, but the average price is about twenty-five dollars per foot.

State and federal laws control all farm programs. Farmers must have licenses. All hides must have serial numbered tags. Because of these controls, alligator poaching has almost been eliminated.

Alligator farms benefit everyone involved. The landowners earn money through the sale of the eggs. Farmers earn money from the alligators they keep, and the hunters and trappers earn money throughout the legal hunting season.

The number of wild alligators has returned to healthy levels. This is because alligator farming has satisfied the huge demand once filled by illegal hunting.

Chapter 5

Saving the Alligator

Alligators are a keystone species. This means they are important to the health of the entire ecosystem. Without alligators, other animals would not survive. In dry weather, smaller animals use the deep holes that alligators dig for water. One animal that benefits from the alligator's hole is the Florida red-bellied turtle. It lays its eggs there.

▶ Habitat Loss

Adult alligators can survive a large amount of water pollution. They can survive the loss of a limb or even a year

▲ Water pollution and flooding in Florida's Everglades has become a threat to the American alligator.

without food.[1] Still, there are limits to what kinds of hardships alligators can face and continue to survive. Alligators face new threats: declining water quality, chemical pollution, and loss of their habitat.[2] In the Everglades, fewer nutrients in the water also threaten the alligator's health.[3]

Wetlands, like the Everglades in Florida, provide important benefits. They act as the home to migratory birds and other endangered species. The Everglades has been drained, and parts of it blocked, for more than fifty years. This was to control floods. These man-made changes have been destroying the alligator's home. The Wetlands Protection Act of 1984 now protects the wetlands.

Loss of the alligator's habitat is also killing its food sources. Rabbits, raccoons, and other small animals are also losing their homes. Loss of habitat in the southern Everglades has caused a decline in wading bird populations. These birds are also vital to the ecosystem. Alligators depend on wading birds for a large part of their diet. Researchers know that alligators living in areas where water has been blocked or diverted (such as the Everglades) are often malnourished and thin.[4]

Runoff

Although lakes may look healthy with flowers and birds, the water may be polluted. Toxic wastes can kill alligators suddenly or slowly over a long period.

In the 1970s, scientists counted almost two thousand alligators in a single night in Lake Apopka, Florida. They thought it would be a good place to harvest alligator eggs. They began collecting the eggs to see how baby alligators would live on farms.

Scientists began to notice fewer babies were hatching from these eggs. They also found that more than 80 percent of the lake's alligators had birth defects.[5] By the late 1980s, only about 150 alligators were left in the lake. Something was wrong.

The lake's water was severely polluted. Human waste and farm chemicals were present. In 1980, there was a huge pesticide spill in the lake. The lake was a chemical soup.[6] In studies, scientists put the same chemicals found in the lake on healthy alligator eggs. The same birth defects showed up in the hatchlings. In some cases, the embryos switched sexes.

"The alligator is a good measure of the water quality," says Paul Cardeilhac, an aquatic-animal veterinarian. "Alligators can live up to seventy years, even in some polluted waters. But their body tissues store the pollution. If the alligators on a lake are in trouble, you'd better take a look at that lake," says Cardeilhac.[7] The pollution in Lake Apopka led scientists to ask some questions. What are we doing to the alligators? What is the price we will have to pay?

▶ Nuisance Alligators

As more people move into the alligator's habitat, it has less room to live. This means alligators wander, looking for water on golf courses and in swimming pools. This is dangerous for people. Many states have decided to create nuisance alligator programs. These programs protect both alligators and people.

Habitat destruction has led to some alligator attacks. The alligators wander and may confuse children and pets for smaller prey. If an alligator threatens a person or a pet, people call a nuisance trapper. The trapper will capture and move the animal to another location. Alligators have a

Because the American alligator is losing more and more of its habitat to humans, it can be found on golf courses and in swimming pools at times. Nuisance alligator programs have been created to remove the animal from these places and relocate them to other areas.

strong homing instinct. The trapper must move the alligator at least thirty miles from its habitat.[8] In Florida, nuisance trappers remove about four thousand alligators each year.[9] Louisiana removed almost 1,400 big alligators in one year. Their average size was over six feet (1.83 m). Removing these few animals does not affect the total number of alligators.

Alligator Attacks on People

In Florida, there are over 1.5 million wild alligators in the wild. There are another two million in Louisiana. There

are so many that occasionally they attack people when they are looking for food.

Normally, alligators do not attack people. When left alone, they will stay away from people. The alligator may have gotten its bad name from being confused with the crocodile. Some crocodiles eat people. Alligators will attack when a person tries to harm its young. Feeding alligators is also very dangerous. Alligators quickly get used to being fed by humans. When the alligator sees a person, it expects food. It will attack a person who does not feed it.

The number of alligators is growing slowly, although the main threat to them is still habitat loss. Some are also caught in fishing nets. Others are run over by cars or boats. People moving into the alligator's habitat, and water pollution, will still threaten its long-term survival, as well. Yet, the alligator has come back from the edge of extinction to flourish in many areas. In a time when more and more species seem to become endangered or threatened, the repopulation of the alligator is a success story.

This series is based on the Endangered and Threatened Wildlife list compiled by the U.S. Fish and Wildlife Service (USFWS). Each book explores an endangered or threatened animal, tells why it has become endangered or threatened, and explains the efforts being made to restore the species' population.

The United States Fish and Wildlife Service, in the Department of the Interior, and the National Marine Fisheries Service, in the Department of Commerce, share responsibility for administration of the Endangered Species Act.

In 1973, Congress took the farsighted step of creating the Endangered Species Act, widely regarded as the world's strongest and most effective wildlife conservation law. It set an ambitious goal: to reverse the alarming trend of human-caused extinction that threatened the ecosystems we all share.

The complete list of Endangered and Threatened Wildlife and Plants can be found at
http://endangered.fws.gov/wildlife.html#Species

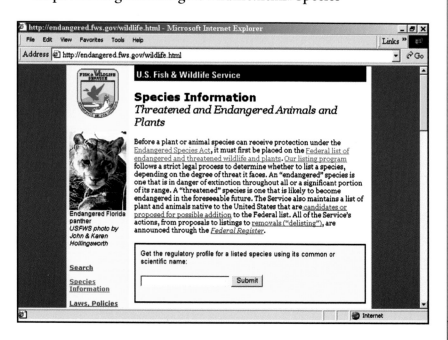

Chapter 1. Prehistoric Monsters

1. Doug Stewart, "Visiting the Heart of Alligator Country," *National Wildlife*, June/July 2000, p. 24.

2. John L. Behler, *National Audubon Society First Field Guide Reptiles* (New York: Scholastic, 1999), p. 46.

Chapter 2. Profile of an Alligator

1. Doug Stewart, "Visiting the Heart of Alligator Country," *National Wildlife*, June/July 2000, p. 22.

2. David Alderton, *Crocodiles and Alligators of the World* (London: Blandford Press, 1991), p. 126.

3. Okefenokee Pastimes, "The Alligator Forecast," *Okefenokee.com*, 1998, <http://www.okefenokee.com/gators.htm> (February 7, 2003).

4. Educational Materials—Teaching to State and National Benchmarks, Louisiana Department of Wildlife and Fisheries, p. 34.

5. Ibid.

6. Danny Goodisman, "Order Crocodilia," *University of Michigan Museum of Zoology, 1995–2003*, <http://animaldiversity.ummz .umich.edu/chordata/reptilia/crocodilia.html> (February 7, 2003).

7. Martha A. Strawn, *Alligators—Prehistoric Presence in the American Landscape* (Baltimore, Md.: The Johns Hopkins University Press, 1997), p. 31.

8. Charles A. Ross, ed., *Crocodiles and Alligators*, (New York: Facts on File, 1989), p. 104.

9. Goodisman, "Order Crocodilia."

10. Ibid.

11. Ibid.

12. Strawn, p. 39.

13. Adam Britton, "Alligator mississippiensis (Daudin, 1801)," *Crocodilian Species List, 1995–2002*, <http://www.flmnh.ufl.edu/ natsci/herpetology/brittoncrocs/csp_amis.htm> (February 7, 2003).

14. Educational Materials—Teaching to State and National Benchmarks, Louisiana Department of Wildlife and Fisheries, p. 34.

15. Anna Maria Gillis, "What Cautionary Tales Can Lake Apopka Tell?" *ZooGoer*, 1995, <http://www.fonz.org/zoogoer/zg1995/lake _apopka_pollution.htm> (February 6, 2003).

16. Jack McClintock, "Alligator," *Discover*, May 2001, p. 52.

17. Strawn, p. 34.

18. Educational Materials—Teaching to State and National Benchmarks, Louisiana Department of Wildlife and Fisheries, p. 34.

19. Britton, *"Alligator mississippiensis (Daudin, 1801)."*

20. Ibid.

21. Strawn, p. 77.

22. Oakland Zoo, "American Alligator," *Animals A-Z*, n.d., <http://www.oaklandzoo.org/atoz/azaligtr.html> (February 6, 2003).

23. Hillary Mayell, "Controlled Alligator Harvest an Effective Conservation Tool, Louisiana Says," *National Geographic News* (sidebar), October 22, 2001, <http://news.nationalgeographic.com/news/2001/10/1022_Ally_1.html> (February 6, 2003).

24. Educational Materials—Teaching to State and National Benchmarks, Louisiana Department of Wildlife and Fisheries, p. 32.

Chapter 3. Alligator Hunting

1. Archie Carr, Ph.D., "Alligators—Dragons in Distress," *National Geographic*, January 1967, p. 147.

2. Vaughn L. Glasgow, *A Social History of the American Alligator*, (New York: St. Martin's Press), 1991, p. 207.

3. Ibid.

4. Ibid., p. 208.

5. Ibid., p. 193.

6. Ibid., p. 195.

7. National Capital Resource Foundation brochure.

8. Ibid.

9. Martha A. Strawn, *Alligators—Prehistoric Presence in the American Landscape* (Baltimore, Md.: The Johns Hopkins University Press, 1997), p. 42.

10. Jim Zumbo, "Dark Waters, Deadly Gators," *Outdoor Life*, February/March 2002, p. 80.

11. Hillary Mayell, "Controlled Alligator Harvest an Effective Conservation Tool, Louisiana Says," *National Geographic News*, October 22, 2001, <http://news.nationalgeographic.com/news/2001/10/1022_Ally_1.html> (February 7, 2003).

12. Ibid.

13. Zumbo, p. 80.

Chapter 4. Alligator Farming

1. Martin P. Masser, "Alligator Production: Breeding and Egg Incubation," *Southern Regional Aquaculture Center*, May 1993, <http://wld.fwc.state.fl.us/gators/farming/231fs.pdf> (February 6, 2003.)

2. Hillary Mayell, "Controlled Harvest an Effective Conservation Tool, Louisiana Says," *National Geographic News*, October 22, 2001, <http://news.nationalgeographic.com/news/2001/10/1022_Ally_1.html> (February 6, 2003).

3. Ibid.

4. Martha A. Strawn, *Alligators—Prehistoric Presence in the American Landscape* (Baltimore, Md.: The Johns Hopkins University Press, 1997), p. 7.

5. Chris Bonura, "New Orleans," *City Business*, November 1, 1999, p. 4.

6. Ibid.

7. Strawn, p. 199.

8. Ibid., p. 200.

Chapter 5. Saving the Alligator

1. Doug Stewart, "Visiting the Heart of Alligator Country," *National Wildlife*, June/July 2000, p. 24.

2. Ibid., p. 22.

3. Ibid., p. 24.

4. National Wildlife Federation, "Alligator mississippiensis," *National Wildlife Federation e-Cards*, 1996–2003, <http://www.nwf.org/everglades/alligator.html> (May 6, 2002).

5. Anna Maria Gillis, "What Cautionary Tales Can Lake Apopka Tell?" *ZooGoer*, 1995, <http://www.fonz.org/zoogoer/zg1995/lake_apopka_pollution.htm> (February 6, 2003).

6. Ibid.

7. Stewart, p. 22.

8. Martha A. Strawn, *Alligators—Prehistoric Presence in the American Landscape* (Baltimore, Md.: The Johns Hopkins University Press, 1997), p. 23.

9. Florida Fish and Wildlife Conservation Commission, "Living With Alligators," *Florida Fish and Wildlife Conservation Commission*, n.d., <http://wld.fwc.state.fl.us/critters/livingwithgators.asp> (February 6, 2003).

Further Reading

Books

Arnosky, Jim. *All About Alligators.* New York: Scholastic, Inc. 1994.

Behler, John and Deborah. *Alligators and Crocodiles.* Stillwater, Minn.: Voyageur Press, Inc., 1998.

Berger, Melvin and Gilda. *Snap! A Book about Alligators and Crocodiles.* New York: Scholastic, Inc., 2001.

Dudley, Karen. *Alligators and Crocodiles.* Austin, Tex.: Raintree Steck-Vaughn Publishers, 1998.

Fitzgerald, Patrick. J. *Croc and Gator Attacks.* Danbury, Conn.: Children's Press, 2000.

Markle, Sandra. *Outside and Inside Alligators.* New York: Antheneum Books for Young Readers, 1998.

Sacks, Janet. *Crocs and Gators.* New York: Penguin Putnam Books for Young Readers, 2001.

Videos

Alligators. International Video Projects, Inc. Coral Gables, Fla.: International Video Projects, 1990.

Gators, crocs and other yucky swamp creatures. Produced by Steve Greenberg and Joel Kaplan. Pembroke Pines, Fla.: Belching Camel Productions, Inc., 1999.

Leaping Lizards. Wildvision/BBC Lionheart production in association with Time/Life Video and Television. Alexandria, Va.: Time Life Video, 1992.

Index

Fishermen's Eye Gallery
239 Lincoln Street
Sitka, AK. 99835
907 747 6080

Invoice# 22451

1	FOSTER BOOKS # 1349	10.00
1	Feast of the Animals # 6421	30.00

October 6, 2012	Subtotal	40.00
	Tax	2.00
VC/#1	Total	42.00
VISA	Tendered	42.00
		.00

X------------------------------
  Signature   42 VISA
I agree to pay above total
 amount according to card
issuer agreement.

Thank you!
online soon
www.fishermenseye.com
Customer Copy